Heinemann
LIBRARY

behind the news | **WAR ON TERROR**: is the world a safer place**?**

GARY E. BARR

www.heinemann.co.uk/library

Visit our website to find out more information about Heinemann Library books.

To order:

☎ Phone 44 (0) 1865 888112

🖹 Send a fax to 44 (0) 1865 314091

💻 Visit the Heinemann bookshop at www.heinemann.co.uk/library to browse our catalogue and order online.

First published in Great Britain by Heinemann Library, Halley Court, Jordan Hill, Oxford OX2 8EJ, part of Harcourt Education.

Heinemann Library is a registered trademark of Harcourt Education Ltd.

Editorial: Andrew Farrow and Richard Woodham
Design: David Poole and Kamae Design
Picture Research: Ruth Blair and Natalie Gray
Production: Huseyin Sami

Originated by Modern Age
Printed and bound in China by South China Printing Company

10-digit ISBN 0 431 11475 7
13-digit ISBN 978 0 431 11475 0
11 10 09 08 07
10 9 8 7 6 5 4 3 2 1

British Library Cataloguing in Publication Data
Barr, Gary E.
War on terror: is the world a safer place?. - (Behind the news)
363.3'25
A full catalogue record for this book is available from the British Library.

Acknowledgements
The publishers would like to thank the following for permission to reproduce photographs:
Corbis pp. 8 (Corbis/Per Wilkund), 10 (Antoine Gyori/AGP), 14 (Reuters), 17 (Reuters), 30 (Ali Abbas/epa), 31 (Namir Noor-Eldeen/Reuters), 34 (Reuters), 42 (Sergio Barrenechea/epa), 45 (Toby Melville/Reuters); Don Wright, The Palm Beach Post, Florida p. 19; Empics pp. 4 (Andrew Medichini/AP), 20 (AP/Tomas Van Houtryve), 37 (Muhammed Muheisen/AP), 43 (AP); Getty Images pp. 5 (AFP), 7 (News), 12 (AFP), 13 (News), 21 (News), 22 (Photo courtesy of Washington Post via Getty Images), 24 (News), 27 (News), 28 (News), 29 (News), 33 (News), 35 (News), 36 (AFP), 38 (News), 40 (News), 44 (News), 46 (News), 47 (AFP/Thomas Lohnes), 49 (Getty Images/Photodisc).

Cover photograph of a soldier in Iraq, reproduced with permission of Corbis (Patrick Robert).

The author and Publishers gratefully acknowledge the publications from which the longer written sources in the book are drawn. In some cases the wording or sentence structure has been simplified to make the material appropriate for a school readership:

Al-Jazeera p.4; BBC Information Service pp. 32, 36; Williamson Murray, *The Iraq War: A Military History* (Cambridge, MA: Harvard University Press, 2003) p.29; *Pittsburgh Post-Gazette* p.5; *Sydney Morning Herald* p.9; *Time* magazine p.33; the *Washington Post* p.18.

CONTENTS

Any words appearing in the text in bold, **like this**, are explained in the glossary.

On 4 February 2005 Giuliana Sgrena, a female Italian journalist, was kidnapped in Iraq. Giuliana was released by her captors on 4 March 2005. As she was being moved to safety, US troops opened fire. Sgrena was wounded and an Italian intelligence officer, Nicola Calipari, was killed.

Differing newspaper reports

The story was news across the world. It was a major event during the occupation of Iraq and the War on Terror by US, British, and other **Coalition** forces. The Arab satellite news channel al-Jazeera and a US newspaper called the *Pittsburgh Post-Gazette* reported the story, but in different ways. Here are excerpts from each:

Al-Jazeera

"Former Italian **hostage** Giuliana Sgrena, shot and wounded by US forces after being freed in Iraq, says she may have been deliberately targeted."

"…Sgrena told Sky Italia TV it was possible the soldiers had targeted her because Washington opposes Italy's dealings with kidnappers that may include ransom payments."

"The US military says the car was speeding towards a checkpoint and ignored warning shots, an explanation denied by government ministers and the driver of the car."

Giuliana Sgrena was held hostage for a month. For both the hostage and loved ones, this is an extremely difficult situation. Giuliana's emotions went from joy, at being released, to horror, when US soldiers mistakenly fired on her car.

Pittsburgh Post-Gazette

"Giuliana Sgrena does not lack a sense of self-importance. The 56-year-old journalist for the Italian communist newspaper *Il Manifesto* thinks she knows so many deep dark secrets the U.S. military tried to shut her up permanently."

"On the night of March 4, their vehicle approached a checkpoint near Baghdad International Airport. The car did not stop. U.S. troops opened fire. Nicola Calipari was killed, Sgrena was slightly wounded."

The truth

Why were the stories reported so differently? Which story is most accurate? It's difficult to know, isn't it? We rely on newspapers and other forms of **media** to give us information about the conflict. As we can see from the reports, however, the news is not always reported in the same way. This is because strong opinions exist concerning the War on Terror, and people see events differently. Some people think it is important to fight the War on Terror, but others do not agree with some of the things that are being done.

Unfortunately, even children have to be searched at checkpoints. Sometimes terrorists use young people to help them carry out attacks. This checkpoint is in Fallujah, Iraq.

Terrorism and 9/11

Terrorism can be defined as attempts to scare people into taking certain actions. By threatening to kill innocent people, terrorists hope national leaders will meet their demands. When they kill, or cause destruction, terrorists want people to be afraid of future violence. Terrorists want to use this fear in order to achieve their goals. Almost all acts of terrorism are carried out in secret – unlike a **conventional war**.

War is declared

The War on Terror started after terrorists from the Middle East attacked in the United States on 11 September 2001 (9/11). Aeroplanes filled with fuel were crashed into buildings in New York City and Washington, D.C., causing thousands of casualties. Nine days after this horrific attack President Bush declared war on terrorists. In a speech on 20 September 2001 he said, "Our war on terror begins with **al-Qaeda** [the terrorist group responsible for the 9/11 attacks] . . . " He continued by saying that US forces would hunt down and bring to justice all terrorist enemies of the United States.

9/11 – the plan

Al-Qaeda terrorists trained for years in Afghanistan and secretly in the United States to carry out the 9/11 attacks. The plan was to destroy important buildings in New York associated with the US economy and significant buildings in Washington, D.C., involved with the US government. By killing large numbers of Americans and destroying important buildings they hoped to punish the United States for supporting Israel – an Arab enemy in the Middle East. The attacks were also a way to protest against US involvement in the **Persian Gulf War** of 1991. Finally, al-Qaeda wanted to show its anger at the United States for establishing military bases in Middle East nations such as Saudi Arabia.

On the morning of 11 September 2001 the terrorists boarded passenger planes in Boston, New York, and Washington that were bound for New York, Los Angeles, and Washington, D.C. They used small, concealed weapons to attack the flight crews and **hijack** the planes.

The terrorists in control of the planes were on **suicide missions**. Large passenger planes carry a tremendous amount of fuel. The terrorists knew that crashing the planes into buildings would cause huge explosions, large fires, death, and destruction.

The attacks

The twin skyscrapers of New York's World Trade Center were over 100 storeys high. At the time, they were two of the tallest skyscrapers in the world. Flight 11 struck the north building at 8:45 a.m.; the south building was struck by Flight 175 at 9:03 a.m. The intense fires of burning jet fuel weakened both structures. First one, and then the other, tower collapsed due to this weakening. Both towers were completely destroyed with thousands of employees and rescue workers inside.

At 9:40 a.m. a third plane – Flight 77 – crashed into the Pentagon in Washington, D.C. This huge building houses the headquarters of the US military. A portion of the five-sided structure was badly damaged by explosion and fire. Almost 200 people lost their lives.

It is thought that the fourth plane – Flight 93 – was headed towards another target in Washington, D.C. Passengers heard about the other terrorist attacks through radios and mobile phones. A group of these passengers heroically attacked the terrorist crew to stop them. Apparently in the struggle to take control of the plane, it crashed in a field in Somerset County, Pennsylvania. There were no survivors.

Most photos showed the World Trade Center collapsing from above. This is a "ground view". Dust sweeps towards people after one huge tower comes down. The 9/11 terrorists had studied how to crash their planes in order to make the buildings collapse.

Bombing in Bali

On 12 October 2002 two explosions ripped apart clubs on the Indonesian island of Bali. These terrorist attacks killed 202 people, including 88 Australians. Australian and Indonesian newspapers reacted strongly – as did their citizens. Most of the victims were in their 20s or 30s and were on holiday in Bali, a South Pacific Island with beautiful beaches. It was the deadliest terrorist attack in Indonesian history. Several Indonesians were tried, convicted, and received the death penalty for these 2002 attacks in Bali. They were members of an **extremist** organization similar to al-Qaeda.

Fires raged after a car bomb exploded outside a bar in Bali. Terrorists targeted this nightspot and another bar because they were popular with Australians and Europeans – both considered enemies. Terrorists know that innocent civilians are easy to attack.

Terrorist methods

Terrorism is used to scare people into taking certain actions or is an extreme reaction meant to punish others. It seems that the Bali bombings were both. The group using the bombs wanted to scare people into not supporting the War on Terror, and to punish people from countries that did support it.

The bombs used in the Bali bombings were electronically operated, hidden in backpacks, and placed in cars. The devices were small, but very powerful. Bombs are a favourite method of terrorists, but there are several others. Kidnapping, hijacking, and publicized threats are also used.

Rather than engaging their enemies in fights out in the open, terrorists choose to secretly carry out missions. Often they are not powerful enough to engage in a conventional war. Terrorists frequently attack civilians and the weak so that people hearing about attacks will be afraid. The terrorists hope that this fear will encourage people to put pressure on their governments to give in to terrorist demands.

THE AUSTRALIAN VIEW

This news report about the Bali bombings appeared in Australia's *Sydney Morning Herald*:
"At 23:05 on 12 October 2002, an electronically triggered bomb hidden in a backpack ripped through Paddy's Bar. The device was small and crude. . . Approximately ten to fifteen seconds later, a second much more powerful car bomb of close to 1,000 kg, . . . was detonated by remote control in front of the Sari Club . . . Scenes of horror and panic inside and outside the bars followed. . . The local hospital was unable to cope with the number of injured, particularly burn victims."

Hard feelings

The way news is reported in one country can influence the opinions of people in another. Australians resented the lack of coverage of the Bali bombings by US newspapers. A few days after the attacks, US newspapers devoted very little space to the disaster. In Australia, meanwhile, the story continued to dominate the front pages.

When 9/11 occurred in the United States, Australian newspapers covered the story for many days. Many Australians resented that newspapers in the United States did not seem to care as much about the Bali bombings. Such disagreements about media coverage can sometimes damage relationships between nations.

"Terrorists Assault a Russian School"

Terrorists come from many nations and cultures, but all use violence or threats of violence as weapons. Extremists from a region of Russia called Chechnya used such tactics in 2004.

In September 2004, primary schoolchildren and teachers in the Russian republic of Chechnya were taken hostage by terrorists. Chechnya wanted Russia to grant it independence so that it could form its own government. Russia had resisted this for many years.

By threatening to kill the schoolchildren unless their demands were met, they hoped to force Russian leaders to submit. The crisis ended in violence on 3 September when shooting suddenly erupted between the hostage-takers and Russian forces. Over 300 civilians were killed and hundreds of others wounded. Of the dead, 186 were schoolchildren. This incident, and others, made Russia willing to take part in the War on Terror.

Flowers and drink bottles pay tribute to victims killed in this Russian school gymnasium. In addition to bullets, a fire erupted adding to the death toll. The hostages had been held for three days in this Beslan school.

History of terrorism

Terrorism has been used for thousands of years in places around the world. In the 20th century, it became particularly effective because of modern media. Extensive media coverage allows terrorist groups to get their messages to people quickly and vividly. Televised pictures of loved ones being threatened have a strong effect, and increase the pressure on leaders to submit to terrorist demands.

Some people immediately think of Arab nations when they hear the word "terrorist". The Middle East, where most Arabs live, has been very troubled in recent years. Clashes involving oil, religion, and differences in **culture** have been common since the 1970s. During that time, however, many terrorist attacks have occurred in nations around the world with no connection to Arabs or the Middle East.

Recent terrorist groups of importance

Al-Qaeda is now one of the most famous terrorist groups. It is thought to have formed in Afghanistan, where Osama Bin Laden quickly became an important leader. For several years, al-Qaeda tried to overthrow the leaders of Saudi Arabia. Bin Laden and other members of al-Qaeda felt Saudi leaders had betrayed **Muslims** by trading and cooperating with the US government.

The Irish Republican Army (IRA) in Northern Ireland, Euskadi ta Askatasuna (ETA) in Spain, and Islamic Jihad are well-known terrorist groups. Each organization has engaged in terrorist attacks and bombings hoping national governments would give in to their demands. Some, such as the IRA, have made peace with their opponents, while the ETA and Islamic Jihad still threaten to use violence. Currently there is controversy about how extensively nations should negotiate with terrorists, but in some cases talks brought peace.

SOME SIGNIFICANT TERRORIST ATTACKS SINCE 1963

Year	Terrorist act	Result
1963	Church bombing during the US Civil Rights movement	4 African-American girls killed
1972	Israeli athletes taken hostage at Olympic Games in Germany	11 athletes killed
1988	Terrorists explode a bomb on a passenger plane over Lockerbie, Scotland	270 killed
1995	Terrorists explode bomb filled with deadly sarin gas in a Tokyo subway	12 killed and 5–6,000 injured
1995	Two US citizens explode a bomb in Oklahoma City	149 workers and 19 children killed

The 9/11 terrorists

The United States and the world were in shock after the 9/11 attacks. TV cameras showed many horrible sights involved in the assaults, including the collapse of the World Trade Center's Twin Towers. As they watched, people were sick with sorrow and furious at the same time. They wanted to know how this could have happened. Who committed this mass murder? The plot was soon traced to Osama Bin Laden and al-Qaeda.

The 9/11 attacks were planned primarily by six al-Qaeda members. Four of these members also piloted the planes: Mohammed Atta, Marwan al-Shehhi, Ziad Jarrah, and Hani Hanjour. They died when the planes they controlled were crashed. There were 15 others who boarded the planes with the pilots. They helped seize control of the planes. They also died when the planes were crashed.

Al-Qaeda's leader

Osama Bin Laden is a Saudi Arabian who grew up with great hatred for the United States and **Western culture**. He hated the United States for being Christian and for supporting Israel. He and other terrorists from the Middle East often say they are fighting a **jihad** – a holy war for Muslims. However, most Muslims in the world oppose terrorist attacks, and object to being associated with such terrorist groups.

The origins of al-Qaeda can be traced to the war between Afghanistan and the Soviet Union (1979–89). Bin Laden and others later tried to overthrow Saudi Arabian leaders for trading and cooperating with the United States – particularly during the Persian Gulf War. Bin Laden was soon **exiled**.

It is believed that Osama Bin Laden is hidden near the Pakistan border with Afghanistan. The United States has made several unsuccessful attempts to capture or kill him. Meanwhile, he and his aides threaten to make more attacks on the United States.

Osama eventually returned to Afghanistan. A group called the **Taliban** controlled this country and shared Bin Laden's hatred for Western culture. Bin Laden, who had access to tremendous wealth, contributed millions to the Taliban. In return, the Taliban allowed Bin Laden to acquire weapons and train terrorists in Afghanistan, which became the headquarters of al-Qaeda.

Taliban soldiers pose for a photo. The Taliban regime was not only disliked for protecting terrorists, but also for their treatment of other Afghans. For example, Afghan women were given almost no respect and not even allowed to attend school.

Bin Laden declared war on the United States and Israel in 1996. In a letter sent to his supporters, he wrote: "My Muslim brothers . . . are calling upon your help and asking you to take part in fighting against the enemy – the Americans and the Israelis."

Osama Bin Laden and his followers were responsible for several attacks on United States citizens and interests around the world. They included attacks on US embassies in Kenya and Somalia in 1998 that killed 12 Americans and 200 other people. Al-Qaeda was also connected with the car bomb detonated beneath Tower One of the World Trade Center in 1993.

THE TALIBAN

Extremists called the Taliban changed Afghanistan when they took over in 1996. Taliban leaders claimed to be following **Islam**, but used brutal methods. Afghans, especially women, had little freedom. Leaders regularly used violence against their own people and did little to help Afghanistan's large class of poor people. Using violence and not helping the poor goes against the basic beliefs of Islam. The Taliban gained a bad reputation from both Islamic and non-Islamic nations.

Afghanistan becomes a target

President Bush declared "war on terrorism" shortly after the 9/11 attacks. After key members of the 9/11 terrorist group were traced to Afghanistan, the US military began to **mobilize**. On 20 September 2001 President Bush sent Afghanistan's Taliban leaders a message to surrender al-Qaeda members or face war with the United States.

Several world leaders supported President Bush in stopping terrorist attacks such as 9/11. The United Nations also began to focus on the problem. Once Osama Bin Laden and al-Qaeda members were connected with the 9/11 attacks, Bush asked the United Nations to support his plan to bring those responsible to justice. They approved.

Emotions and actions

A wave of **nationalism** swept the United States and citizens displayed the US flag everywhere. When President Bush called for military forces to be mobilized for war against al-Qaeda and the Taliban government of Afghanistan, Americans whole-heartedly approved. The United States **Congress**, which holds the power to declare war, had previously passed **legislation** to allow the president to take all measures necessary to fight terrorism.

Special forces used helicopters to search for the enemy during the 2001 war with Afghanistan. Such methods are still used.

Readying for war

By 22 September, US warships and planes quickly moved towards Afghanistan. Thousands of troops would follow in ships and other military transports. Their aim was to crush Afghanistan's Taliban government and capture Bin Laden and other members of al-Qaeda.

Afghanistan is a rugged land with many high mountains. For most of its history it has been a poor nation. However, during a conflict in the 1980s its small army and **guerilla** forces fought very hard against Soviet troops. Many Soviet troops were killed and the war became so difficult and costly that the Soviets pulled their forces out. The United States was well aware of the difficulties Soviets had encountered, and prepared for a tough fight.

Over 20 nations sent troops, money, and other assistance in the mission to capture those responsible for the 9/11 attacks. Uzbekistan and Pakistan, as border nations to Afghanistan, became key supporters of the operation. In many ways, the whole world seemed to be joining the United States in a quest for justice.

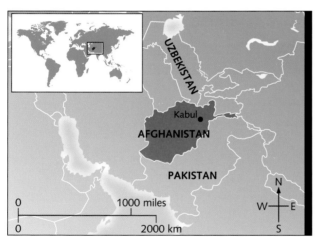

This map shows the location of Afghanistan.

THE DEMANDS OF THE UNITED STATES

"Deliver to United States authorities all the leaders [of al-Qaeda] who hide in your land. Close immediately and permanently every terrorist camp in Afghanistan, and hand over every terrorist, and every person in their support structure, to appropriate authorities . . . The Taliban must act, and act immediately. They will hand over the terrorists, or they will share in their fate."

President Bush, in a speech made to Congress on 20 September 2001

The United States attacks Afghanistan

The war with Afghanistan began with US aircraft launching massive attacks. Ground troops started an invasion and had little trouble defeating Afghan forces. A **democratic government** was established in December 2004, but sporadic fighting continues between terrorists and US forces that still occupy the nation.

Air strikes were launched on 7 October 2001 hitting targets in major Afghan cities. Thirteen days later ground troops invaded from Uzbekistan, located north of Afghanistan. Led by special-forces units, they quickly defeated the opposition and captured the important cities of Kabul and Mazar-e-Sharif, in the north, and Kandahar in the south.

This is how the first attacks on Afghanistan were reported by shianews.com: "Thunderous explosions and the rattle of anti-aircraft fire were heard in the Afghan capital of Kabul on Sunday night as the United States and Britain launched military attacks in Afghanistan. Electricity was shut off throughout the city. 'On my orders, the United States military has begun strikes against al Qaeda training camps and military installations of the Taliban regime,' Bush said. 'We are supported by the collective will of the world.'"

By 2 March 2002 the conventional part of the war was over. Some Taliban and al-Qaeda forces had escaped into high mountains and other hiding places. An intense search for Osama Bin Laden was on, but he went into hiding. The United States and troops from other countries attacked as many terrorist hideouts as possible, but Bin Laden was not found.

Afghanistan rebuilds

The Taliban government collapsed, and many members of al-Qaeda and the Taliban were taken prisoner. Despite this, US troops in Afghanistan continued to find other suspected terrorists in the country for several years. Meanwhile, Afghanistan began to rebuild.

Afghanistan has had a history of **disunity** and these problems persisted until recent years. Poor leadership in government, interference by foreign nations, lack of economic development, and the difficulties of communication in a country divided by rugged mountains have all played a part in keeping Afghans from working together. At the end of the war in 2003, some Afghans still showed more loyalty to regional leaders and local groups than to their nation's leaders.

Painters work on a new building. Afghanistan has suffered countless conflicts during its long history. Wars with ancient conquerors such as Tamerlane and Genghis Khan have been replaced with recent conflicts. Afghans now hope for peace and stability.

Freely elected government

Gradually, US officials worked with regional leaders to form a new government. A popular Afghan leader called Hamid Karzai was chosen to lead a temporary national government in 2001 until elections could be arranged. In October 2004 Karzai defeated several opponents in a **free election**. Schools are being built, businesses are being re-established, and women have regained rights they lost under strict Taliban rule. Although some terrorist attacks still occur, Afghanistan is moving toward a brighter future. Meanwhile, many prisoners captured by the United States during the war were transferred to Guantánamo Bay, Cuba.

DEADLY MINES

Deadly explosives plague Afghanistan. Underground land mines and live explosives are still found. Some mines date back to the time when Soviets invaded, or when Afghan groups fought in the 1990s. In addition, unexploded canisters from US cluster bombs are sometimes discovered. These are very dangerous because some look like empty drink cans to children. US and Canadian units have worked hard to find and destroy these explosives, but there are so many that it may take several years.

Objective reporting and Guantánamo Bay

One of the most important rules for the news media is to report things **objectively**. Newspapers, TV, radio, and other media are supposed to tell people what happened in an accurate way so they will be well informed.

FBI Agents Allege Abuse of Detainees at Guantánamo Bay

The following appeared in an article of the *Washington Post* about prisoners captured during the War on Terror and being held at Guantánamo Bay, Cuba:

"Detainees at the U.S. military prison at Guantanamo Bay, Cuba, were shackled to the floor . . . for more than 24 hours at a time, left without food and water, and . . . FBI agents and officials also said that they witnessed the use of growling dogs at Guantanamo Bay to intimidate detainees . . . in an apparent attempt to soften [their] resistance to [questioning]."

Many other media reports have also described how prisoners were tortured and denied basic human rights. They have carried stories about how US personnel had abused prisoners' copies of the Islamic holy book, the Koran.

Most of the prisoners held at the Guantánamo prison were captured during the war with Afghanistan. Some visitors and observers of the Guantánamo prison claimed the United States was mistreating its captives. The human rights organization Amnesty International has called the prisoners' treatment "a human rights scandal". This treatment went against international conferences and other documents that set up rules for prisoner treatment.

Prisoner treatment

There are rules for how prisoners should be treated. Countries around the world have signed agreements to protect prisoners from abuse.

In 1949 the Geneva Convention set rules for prisoner-of-war treatment. These rules are internationally recognized and very detailed. Other documents, laws, and practices also exist to protect prisoners from unfair treatment.

In 1948 several nations met to form and agree on a Declaration of Human Rights. This document was produced after World War II. During the War, there were numerous instances in which prisoners were tortured. One of the most important quotes in the Declaration dealing with prisoners is: "No one shall be subjected to torture or to cruel, inhuman or degrading treatment."

THE GENEVA CONVENTION

The following are excerpts from the Geneva Convention regarding the treatment of prisoners of war:

- From Article 13 – "Prisoners of war must at all times be humanely treated. Any unlawful act or omission by the Detaining Power causing death or seriously endangering the health of a prisoner of war in its custody is prohibited…"
- From Article 17 – "No physical or mental torture, nor any other form of coercion, may be inflicted on prisoners of war to secure from them information of any kind whatever. Prisoners of war who refuse to answer may not be threatened, insulted, or exposed to any unpleasant or disadvantageous treatment of any kind."

What does this editorial cartoon mean? Cartoonists give opinions by using simple images. The 1949 Geneva Convention was an international agreement that protected war prisoners' rights. This 2006 cartoon expressed opinions about prisoner treatment at Camp X-Ray, Guantánamo Bay.

Recent rules

In 1985 the United Nations held a convention to deal with the issue of torture. It declared that under no circumstances is there "justification of torture". It defined torture as, "any act by which severe pain or suffering, whether physical or mental, is intentionally inflicted on a person".

Nations such as the United States have added to agreements by the international community. In its 1992 US Army Field Manual the following appears: "[The Geneva Convention on rules for war] and U.S. policy expressly prohibit acts of violence or intimidation, including physical or mental torture, threats [or] insults . . . as a means of or aid to interrogation."

Unlawful combatants

There have been many arguments about the status of the prisoners at Guantánamo Bay. The Bush **administration** said the prisoners were "unlawful combatants". This means they do not have rights that would normally be granted to other prisoners. Normally, the US government has to take prisoners before a US judge and say what crime the prisoners are being charged with. This process, called habeas corpus, is a constitutional right in the United States and many other countries. But because the prisoners were being held in Cuba, they did not have this right.

US Secretary of Defense Donald Rumsfeld defended the administration's decisions. He said: " There are among these prisoners people who are perfectly willing to kill themselves and kill other people. Unlawful combatants do not have any rights under the Geneva Convention."

An inmate of Camp X-Ray at Guantánamo Bay, dressed in orange, is escorted by two guards. Other inmates can be seen in their cells.

US Secretary of Defense Donald Rumsfeld inspects a Guantánamo Bay prison. The Bush administration believed prisoners in the War on Terror should have almost no rights, but many US citizens disagreed. The US government has now altered its position.

Actions are louder than words

Many people believe that the example set by the United States is more important than what its leaders say. Mistreating others – whether they are prisoners or not – presents a very negative view to the world's people. In the case of the Guantánamo prisoner treatment, the media fulfilled an important responsibility. In most instances, the media accounts were objective and uncovered problems that need correcting.

Many Americans called for these actions to stop and for detailed investigations to be carried out. In 2005, US Senator John McCain led a vote that set limits on the treatment of prisoners. McCain had been tortured while a prisoner in Vietnam, during the Vietnam War. He described how American prisoners were able to resist the cruelties inflicted on them: "We took great strength from the belief that we were different from our enemies."

Finally, in July 2006, the United States agreed to apply the Geneva Convention to all terrorist suspects in US custody.

Reports and images of prisoner abuse at Abu Ghraib Prison, Iraq, reached people all around the world. Many people were shocked and disgusted by them.

"Turmoil Mounts over Abuse of Iraqi Prisoners"

In 2004, the press and some military leaders released a gruesome report about a US-controlled prison in Iraq. Abu Ghraib prison held Iraqis captured during the war. They were being abused and mistreated, and filmed during their agony. Some of this was being done in an attempt to reveal information about other terrorists and terrorist attacks. However, it appears that some of the abuse was carried out as a disgusting form of entertainment for prison guards. Either way it went against conventions on the treatment of prisoners.

Correcting problems

According to Seymour Hersh, who wrote a story based on US Army Major General Antonio Taguba's report, there was "rampant abuse of Iraqi prisoners" who "were beaten and threatened with . . . electrocution and dog attacks," and other harsh actions. Revelations such as these angered Iraqis and Americans alike and actions were taken to stop such behaviour. By the time Taguba's report was completed, 17 soldiers and officers had been removed from duty, and 6 soldiers faced prison sentences as a result of their roles in the events. However, the reports also led to more problems.

Helping the enemy

Phillip Carter, writing for United Press International, said, "The acts they document have helped to energize the **insurgency** in Iraq [increasing] the risks faced by our soldiers each day." How could reporting the problems that were caused by a few prison guards result in difficulties for Coalition troops?

A common emotion among humans is the desire for revenge. When others, especially friends or loved ones, are badly hurt, people often want to retaliate (hit back). The US military expected members of the insurgency to retaliate. Even more importantly, some Iraqis who formerly supported the efforts of the United States now felt betrayed. Could they trust the United States to be fair?

Bad information

Bias, exaggeration, and unreliable sources are examples of poor reporting. When only one side of a story is told or unreasonable exaggerations are made, the reader isn't getting a true account of what happened. Reliable sources are also important to the accuracy of news. Sources are people who volunteer information to a reporter.

A serious case of improper reporting occurred over a century ago, in 1898. A New York newspaper called THE JOURNAL wanted the United States to go to war with Spain. It published a story about Spanish officials forcing young Cuban women to undress in front of them during a search. The newspaper even had a drawing by an artist they said witnessed this incident. It was revealed later that the story was untrue and the artist wasn't even at the site. Nevertheless, the anger caused by this, and other biased stories in US publications, helped cause the Spanish-American War.

When newspapers get a story wrong they must print a **retraction**. However, the retraction does not have to appear in the same manner as the original story. While the original may have had huge headlines and been positioned on the front page, retractions sometimes appear as very small stories inside the newspaper.

Factual and objective reporting led to important investigations being opened at Abu Ghraib. Some personnel working at the prison faced court trials and punishment. For example, in June 2006 a US Army dog handler was convicted of using his animal to torment a prisoner at the prison. US citizens have also called for an end to similar practices directed towards prisoners in the War on Terror.

Persian Gulf War

Several nations fought in the war against Iraq in 1991. It was called the Persian Gulf War and was caused when Iraq's forces invaded the small nation of Kuwait. Iraq's leader, Saddam Hussein, wanted control of this small, but oil-rich nation and found an excuse to take it. The United States, Britain, and several other nations worked together and quickly defeated Iraq. Kuwait was freed and Hussein's regime was forced to sign a treaty.

"Germany Makes Plea to Prevent War"

Under this treaty Iraq was supposed to get rid of all its major weapons, allow officials to inspect sites where weapons might be stored, and take no action against **surveillance** planes. Iraq resisted these terms time and again and Saddam Hussein and his regime violated the treaty. Specifically, Iraq fired on US planes patrolling the area on numerous occasions and constantly prevented officials from inspecting possible weapons sites.

The Iraqi government became increasingly uncooperative until the United States could take no more. Warnings from the United Nations, the United States, and many other nations went unheeded. Despite this, Germany tried to stop war breaking out because many critics of war believed that the death and destruction caused by war should be the last resort in resolving a crisis.

US Lieutenant General Jeff Conway stands on a tank to address British troops. In March 2003 these soldiers prepared to invade Iraq. British forces captured the important Iraqi port city Basra and secured southern Iraq.

Mixed support

Saddam Hussein's defiance, reports that he was supporting terrorists, and rumours that Iraq was developing nuclear weapons caused the United States to take action.

The United States quickly readied for war and tried to gain **allies**. Britain and a few other countries pledged complete support, but the United Nations, France, Russia, and Germany wanted to find either a peaceful solution or more proof to support the rumours. Meanwhile the United States continued to demand that Saddam Hussein open his military sites to UN inspectors. Hussein refused.

Finally President Bush told the American people that the United States would go to war with Iraq without United Nations approval if necessary. He sent shiploads of US troops into waters near Iraq. Turkey, Syria, and Iran would not permit US ground troops to use their lands for invasion routes. This meant that most US ground troops would have to attack Iraq from Saudi Arabia and Kuwait.

On 18 March 2003, with troops ready to make the assault, Bush sent Saddam Hussein a final ultimatum: comply with all the terms of the treaty he had signed, or face war. Hussein refused again.

BRITISH PRIME MINISTER EXPLAINS SUPPORT FOR THE UNITED STATES

Prime Minister Tony Blair has been criticized for supporting the United States in Afghanistan and Iraq. He said: "My father's generation went through the experience of the Second World War, when Britain was under attack . . . And there was one nation and one people that, above all, stood side by side with us at that time. And that nation was America . . . And I say to you, we stand side by side with you now, without hesitation."

Responses to the attack

On 21 March 2003 www.dawn.com posted an article headed "France, Russia to Challenge Invasion". It said that, "Russia and France on Friday challenged the legal basis of the US-led invasion of Iraq, with Moscow saying it would appeal to the United Nations to rule on the legality of the attack. French President Jacques Chirac said the United States and Britain had breached international law by declaring war on Iraq without a UN mandate. [Russian President Vladimir] Putin . . . called on the United States to stop the attack on Iraq, saying that attack was a 'serious political mistake. . .'"

In China, in January 2003, Beijing's *People's Daily Online* carried the headline "Blair for Iraqi Invasion Without 2nd UN Resolution". A second resolution by the United Nations was needed for the world peacekeeping organization to give approval for war actions against Iraq.

War

Despite much international opposition, on 20 March 2003 a massive air attack by the United States and Britain opened the war in Iraq. British, US, and other Coalition ground forces invaded a few days after the air assault in an attempt to completely crush Saddam Hussein's regime.

In the huge air strikes against Iraq, high-tech missiles were launched from ships in the Persian Gulf, while fighter planes hit other targets. Baghdad and major Iraqi cities' power plants and communications facilities were quickly destroyed. The precise, high-tech weapons caused very few Iraqi civilians to be casualties, while inflicting heavy losses on Iraqi troops.

Ground troops attack

On 21 March 2003 Coalition ground troops crossed into Iraq. Most entered from Kuwait and Saudi Arabia and moved north. The Iraqi Army was no match for the superior weapons of Coalition forces, which could shoot further and more accurately. Iraq had no air force to defend itself, but there were furious battles in some of the cities.

The city of An Nasariyah, located in central Iraq, was difficult for US forces to capture and much street fighting occurred there. Meanwhile, British forces moved quickly through southern Iraq into Basra, the second-largest city and best seaport. Suddenly Iraqi troops erupted with heavy gunfire against the British, but this opposition was short-lived.

Egyptian university students protest the US-led war against Iraq. Though it believes in freedom of religion, US culture is dominated by Christian ideals. Some followers of Islam wonder if US attacks are being made in part because of religious differences.

Victory?

Even with these pockets of resistance, it only took a month before US tanks rolled into Baghdad, Iraq's capital. On 14 April President Bush declared that the major fighting in the war was over.

Many of those loyal to Saddam Hussein or who were strongly opposed to the United States fled, but some went into hiding and fought on. The resulting conflict between these fighters and the United States became known as the insurgency. At first there were small, scattered attacks, but the movement grew and eventually caused destruction, disruption, and large numbers of deaths in Iraq.

ARAB OPINIONS

These excerpts from Arab newspapers illustrate some of the views of the Arab world:

Al Quds is an Arab newspaper published in Jerusalem. On 25 March 2003 it published an article headed "Who will lose this War?" It said the losers in the Iraq war were: 1. International law – it was a war with no justification; 2. Democracy – there was no respect for the people's opinion; 3. Mothers, wives, and children – who lose loved ones; 4. Earth's environment – because of the destruction that would occur.

Al-Seyassah, a newspaper published in Kuwait, wrote on 24 March 2003, "huge demonstrations…were organized in… the Arab world demanding the withdrawal of American forces… These demonstrators… didn't budge when the despotic regime in Iraq killed more than 5,000 citizens in Kurdish Halabja, Iraq."

Al-Thawra, a newspaper in Baghdad, said on 20 March 2003, "The first loss of the American 'Administration of Evil' is the International isolation it will suffer."

In combat

Satellites and other communication technology meant that countless "on-the-spot" reports were made during the war in Iraq. Using accounts of **embedded reporters**, who accompanied troops as they fought, is not a new idea. However, hearing and seeing these reports in live broadcasts was new. Camera phones and other equipment beamed live images around the world.

Advantages and disadvantages

Such reporting gave viewers immediate, up-close descriptions of military operations. People could see and hear exactly what was happening. Critics have pointed out several disadvantages of embedded reporters. In combat, troops may be hampered by having to protect these journalists. Also, since most reporters and viewers are not professionally trained military staff, misunderstandings can easily occur.

An embedded reporter takes notes. Charles Crain was reporting for *Time* magazine during a battle against Iraqi insurgents in 2005. Critics feel that embedded reporters hamper soldiers, who have to protect the reporters.

Dangerous city

An Nasiriyah was a key city for US forces to control as they moved towards Baghdad and some vivid on-the-spot accounts were filed. At An Nasiriyah, the bulk of the invading force had to cross the Euphrates River. Buildings close to main roads were good places for Iraqi troops to hide and ambush US troops as they went past.

After securing safe crossings through An Nasiriyah, US troops quickly moved north. Near Karbala they were stopped again. Located only 100 kilometres (60 miles) south of Baghdad, supplies for troops were running low. In addition, Iraq's best fighting unit, called the Republican Guard, now faced them.

Closing in

The road to Baghdad split, with one part crossing a river to a city called Al Hillal. Another road passed through a mountain gap to the city of Karbala. Furious fighting took place for almost a week, but US forces won and moved on to the outskirts of Baghdad. Tanks soon moved through the heart of Iraq's capital city with little resistance.

Celebrations broke out and most residents of Baghdad, happy to be rid of Saddam Hussein's brutal reign, gave US troops a warm welcome. The most spectacular celebration occurred when residents pulled down a huge statue of Saddam. Everything appeared to be going well, but some Iraqis were not finished fighting.

Preparations are made to pull down a statue of Saddam Hussein in Baghdad. Ruthless dictators such as Saddam held power by limiting people's freedom and by using force.

AN ACCOUNT OF THE FIGHTING

This account is taken from a book called *The Iraq War: a Military History*, which combines embedded reports, military reports, and interviews:
". . .helicopters spotted six troop-carrying vehicles and two tanks defending a bridge near An Nasiriyah. They launched missiles and destroyed the vehicles. An hour later an armored unit followed up the helicopter attacks and assaulted the bridge across the Euphrates. Following this came the advance forces of the 3rd Infantry Division. They took control of the bridge after two hours of fighting with Iraqi ground troops . . . Combat Teams used this bridge to advance north into Iraq."

"Anti-US Attacks in Iraq More Effective"

How could Coalition forces win a swift, one-sided victory only to suffer large numbers of casualties afterwards? Sometimes the toughest opponents are ones that are small and unseen. It is very difficult to identify fighters who look like good Iraqi citizens. Small bombs can cause extensive damage and many deaths. The combination of these factors with fighters that strongly believed in their cause has resulted in a devastating insurgency.

Death then more death

Coalition forces suffered fewer than 200 deaths during the war in Iraq. Most of Iraq's top government and military officials were captured in the months after the war. Then on 13 December 2003 Saddam Hussein was captured. Despite this, the insurgency grew.

Unfortunately, terrorist attacks afterwards caused much more death, destruction, and disruption among Iraqis and Coalition forces than the war itself. By March 2006 over 2,300 US soldiers had lost their lives during the insurgency. Britain and other allies experienced similar increases, although their totals were lower because they had fewer troops in the area. Iraqi civilians have suffered the most casualties. Over 10,000 were killed during insurgent terrorist acts between 2003 and 2006.

Insurgents destroyed a five-storey hotel in Baghdad in March 2004. Their weapon was a powerful car bomb. Twenty-seven people died and forty were wounded in the attack.

Why insurgency?

Those who took part in the insurgency did so for various reasons. Some strongly disapproved of the war and of the United States. Others wanted more say in the new government of Iraq. Some still supported Saddam Hussein. A few had criminal motives. At first there were a few isolated attacks, mostly against US troops. As time went on, however, more attacks occurred and there were more assaults against Iraqis who supported plans for a new democratic government.

Terrorists came into Iraq from other nations. Most had connections to al-Qaeda or other organizations that hated the United States. They have been involved in significant terrorist acts that killed large numbers of Iraqi civilians and Coalition troops. Kidnappings, roadside bombs, ambushes, **suicide car bombs**, and televised executions were carried out.

Executing the innocent

Members of the insurgency brought more pressure on Coalition leaders by taking hostages. If their demands were not met, they sometimes killed innocent victims and filmed the executions. Images that show violent deaths of innocent hostages were horrible for loved ones to witness. The media had a responsibility to report the news, but publicizing such actions helped kidnappers and terrorists influence people. If there had been no media coverage would there have been as many kidnappings?

Economic damage

Insurgents have had much success disrupting Iraq's economy. Oil pipelines, electric power plants, and other major facilities were secretly bombed numerous times by terrorists. The ultimate hope of insurgents is to disrupt and scare Iraqis and loved ones of those serving in Iraq to the point that Coalition forces would be pulled out.

Young insurgents display a rocket launcher. However, an enemy is difficult to identify when for most of the time it does not carry weapons.

"Spain threatens Iraq troop pull-out"

On 15 March 2004, the BBC reported that, "Spain's Socialist Party prime minister-elect says he will pull troops out of Iraq – unless the UN takes charge. Jose Luis Rodriguez Zapatero said: 'The war in Iraq was a disaster, the occupation of Iraq is a disaster.' He called for a grand international alliance against terror and an end to 'unilateral wars'."

Opposition from the Middle East

From the beginning, most nations of the Middle East were concerned about the invasion of Iraq. There had been many negative attitudes towards Arab and other peoples in the area for several years. Although many Arab countries were opposed to the Iraqi regime, they did not want Western powers to have a greater influence in the region. Now it seemed that the United States would be in control of one of their Arab neighbours.

There were fears among many people in the Middle East about the United States spreading the conflict to nearby lands or imposing its religion and culture. Terrorists operating in the Middle East warned that these things would occur. Despite assurances from the United States, a great number of people in the region remain **sceptical**.

Opposition outside the Middle East

Opposition to the war was not limited to the Middle East. European nations that had been willing allies in the war in Afghanistan and in numerous other crises were strongly opposed to the war in Iraq. Many hard feelings developed between the United States and nations such as France, Russia, and Germany. Many protestors filled the streets of European countries condemning US military actions in Iraq.

Several people accused President Bush of trying to capture the huge supplies of oil found in Iraq, or of seeking revenge for his father's failure to achieve a complete victory over Iraq in the Persian Gulf War. President Bush's father, George H. Bush, had led the United States to victory in 1991 against Saddam Hussein's forces and expelled them from Kuwait, but had decided not to completely conquer Iraq.

Protests in Coalition nations

Some allies remained loyal and sent troops and other aid to help the United States win the war. When hostages were taken and in some cases executed by terrorists during the insurgency, some nations recalled their troops.

Prime Minister Tony Blair, Australia's Prime Minister John Howard, and others remained supportive of the United States in the Iraq war and the subsequent occupation. This support remained despite strong protests by citizens in their respective countries.

Thousands of Italians protest the war in Iraq. Demonstrators in numerous countries blamed President Bush for ongoing violence in Iraq and the Middle East. About 150,000 people took part in 2004.

FOR AND AGAINST THE WAR

On 18 July 2005, *Time* magazine reported on two opposing views on the war in Iraq:

Charles Krauthammer, an award-winner writer for the *Washington Post*, said, "The US is supporting a new antiterrorist government in Afghanistan, hunting Al Qaeda in mountain hideaways of Pakistan, cooperating with countries around the world to disrupt terrorism and its funding. How has the War in Iraq caused us to be more unsafe?"

Daniel Benjamin, a Senior Fellow in the Center for Strategic and International Studies, said, " Radical Islamic groups predicted that the US would impose its culture on the Middle East. With the invasion of Iraq, their predictions appear to have come true and built up much hatred. Iraq has inspired extremists around the world to come to Iraq…"

UN weapons inspectors search a suspected site for Iraqi WMD. This photo was taken over a year before the war began. Inspectors were barred from examining many similar locations. This made US leaders feel Saddam had hidden the WMD.

Weapons of mass destruction?

Weapons of mass destruction (WMD) are ones that can cause thousands of deaths in an instant. President Bush said that the threat of weapons of mass destruction was the main reason the United States needed to go to war with Iraq. Despite rumours, no weapons of mass destruction have been found in Iraq.

The US Congress and American people supported the war because of President Bush's allegations. The President and Secretary of State Colin Powell presented testimony that Iraq was supporting terrorists, data about Saddam Hussein's brutality to Iraqis, and evidence of WMD.

Since no WMD had been found in previous UN inspections, France, Germany, and Russia were hesitant to go to war. They agreed that if WMD were found and Saddam refused to give them up, action should be taken, but they would not support war in March 2003.

Searching

The United States made an extensive search for Iraq's WMD after major fighting in the war had stopped. For over a year hundreds of sites were closely examined for any sign of these weapons, but none were found. A few officials believed that Iraq had WMD, which it transported to other countries when a US invasion became a threat. No proof of this has ever been discovered.

In January 2005 the Bush administration finally admitted that there were no WMD in Iraq. They said that faulty reports by spies led to these inaccuracies. Officials from both the United States and Britain were involved in the inaccurate reports.

TYPES OF WMD

- Atomic bombs – One dropped on Hiroshima, Japan, in 1945 killed approximately 75,000 people instantly, but modern weapons are much more powerful. They kill with a combination of intense heat, explosive power, and air-poisoning gases.
- Biological weapons – kill with poisonous substances found in nature. For example, by releasing certain bacteria into a city reservoir, thousands of people could be killed by drinking household water.
- Chemical weapons – During World War I, mustard gas was used to kill hundreds of soldiers. Cannons propelled shells towards the enemy lines. Filled with chemicals such as mustard gas, they exploded and spread gases among enemy troops. Some troops died quickly after inhaling the gas, but many others slowly suffocated – often taking a month to die.
- Radiological weapons – kill by spreading poisonous substances in the air. They are sometimes called "dirty bombs". They work in a similar way to nuclear weapons, but are simpler, easier to make, and less explosive.

Painful mistake

US Secretary of State Colin Powell presented evidence to the United Nations. He showed photographs of suspected WMD sites and stressed the need for action against Iraq. The material was found to be inaccurate. Powell said, "Of course it will [tarnish my image]. It's a blot. I'm the one who presented it on behalf of the United States to the world, and [it] will always be a part of my record. It was painful. It's painful now."

Powell shows a video to the United Nations supporting his allegations of WMD. This claim turned out to be based on faulty information.

Iraqis speak

Life was difficult for most Iraqis under Saddam Hussein. He ruled from 1979 to 2003 and allowed little freedom, permitted no opposition, and harshly punished any who disagreed. Despite being rich with oil, a small percentage of Iraqis controlled almost all of the wealth. Hussein kept much wealth for himself and built lavish palaces for personal use. Almost all Iraqis celebrated his removal and subsequent trial.

Life under Saddam

In a BBC article entitled "After the War: Iraqis Face New Lives", some Iraqi opinions were expressed:

"Saad, a 32 year-old engineer from Basra said, 'Let me describe our situation before the fall of the previous regime. We were like a sick, weak prisoner under the thumb of a cruel jailer . . . The previous regime used to tell us what to read, what to watch and what to listen to. Iraqis are feeling better. They are breathing the air of freedom.'"

Insurgency

Unfortunately, violence caused during the insurgency killed thousands of Iraqi civilians. To show their displeasure, terrorists killed scores of Iraqis who worked in government positions. Police and government officials were common targets. However, no one was safe – innocent adults and children were sometimes killed while shopping, or even while they worshipped.

"'As an Iraqi, I see lack of security as the most important problem,' said Noura, a computer specialist from Baghdad. 'Many Iraqis use their new freedom ... in a selfish way. Many do not respect the law.'"

A sad sight in any conflict is that of civilian refugees. These Kurdish people were trying to escape fighting that occurred between Iraqi and Kurdish forces in 1991. US, French, and British troops mounted an operation and helped save 500,000 Kurdish refugees.

Civil war?

At times there were so many violent acts and signs of instability that outsiders thought Iraq might have a civil war. According to the BBC article, "Kaban, who works in electronics, said, 'Many people predicted a civil and ethnic war between Iraqis would erupt, but the Iraqis were the first to sense the danger and ensured that it would never happen.'"

Several groups with differing beliefs including **Sunnis**, **Shi'ites**, and **Kurds** needed to unite for Iraq to be successful, and government leaders had to gain the trust of their people.

OPPOSING GROUPS

There are deep divisions between Sunni and Shi'ite Muslims in Iraq. Under Saddam Hussein the Sunni Muslims controlled the government even though Shi'ites were a larger group. Since the new government of Iraq was democratic and allowed majority rule, Sunnis lost power. Some Sunnis have resorted to violence to try to regain power, because they oppose United States involvement, and because of old arguments with Shi'ite Muslims.

Kurds live in northern Iraq and parts of Turkey. Many Kurds believe that they should have their own nation. They are not Arab and have their own customs and beliefs.

A Baghdad family watches President Bush on their Iraqi news station. The station called Al Arabiya broadcast Bush's speech. In his speech, Bush expressed his opposition to the prisoner abuses that took place in Abu Ghraib prison.

The world after 9/11

"In the globalized world, the US can no longer behave as if problems of the rest of the world need not bother it." This quote, from Deccanherald.com, gives the opinion of Indian senior UN official and author Shashi Tharoor after the 9/11 attacks.

The most common comment of US adults concerning 9/11 is that "the whole world has changed". Why do they say this?

Keeping civilians safe from terrorist attacks suddenly became a primary goal for governments. In the United States, the federal government established a new department for that purpose: The Department of Homeland Security. During 2003 Britain passed measures designed to deal with terrorist attacks. They gave the government power to deny certain freedoms to suspected terrorists during times of crisis. Australia and other nations also enacted tougher laws to prevent attacks.

Several US government agencies were combined into the Department of Homeland Security. Its priorities are: 1. Improving the ability to share information and resources among different agencies; 2. Centralized decision-making; 3. Employing government agents who can focus on anti-terrorism issues.

Britain passed the Terrorism Act 2000 and the Anti-Terrorism, Crime, and Security Act 2001 as anti-terrorism legislation. These laws give police much more power if they suspect a person may be a terrorist. They have expanded "stop and search powers" and can detain suspected terrorists from 48 hours to 7 days with the permission of a magistrate. Under certain conditions at the national level, the home secretary can indefinitely detain a foreign terrorist suspect.

New York City policemen attempt to prevent a terrorist attack. Radiation detectors scan a lorry before it travels on the George Washington Bridge. These instruments can find poisonous substances and certain items that could be used for explosives.

New security measures

In general, new priorities were put in place. Increased searches and security were put in place at airports, train stations, skyscrapers, government buildings, and at events where large crowds gather. In the United States, guarding borders became more important to prevent potential terrorists from sneaking into the country. Security was tightened at power plants, city water supplies, and at places where dangerous chemicals were present.

An alert system was started. Depending on the colour announced, a city or the whole nation takes certain actions. The colours are green, blue, yellow, orange, and red. The closer the colour is to red, the more serious the threat is of a terrorist attack.

High costs

Almost everyone agrees that countries need to increase their vigilance, but homeland security is expensive. It takes large numbers of employees to check everyone in crowded places, to examine cargos on huge ships, or to guard long borders. In the year 2000 about US$13 billion was spent on homeland security in the United States. By 2006, the nation was spending approximately US$50 billion for the same purpose.

The job of homeland security is so big and so expensive that many questions remain about how best to spend money and what security is most important. Some US cities have complained that it costs them large amounts of money when the homeland security alerts become elevated. This is because the system requires cities to have extra police and other personnel working during high-alert situations. Having extra personnel on duty means that cities have to pay out extra wages.

The United States has not experienced a major terrorist attack since 9/11 and officials have uncovered numerous terrorist plots. However, most Americans believe that homeland security has many limitations and that another attack is inevitable.

"Terror Laws 'Eat Away at Privacy'"

A 2004 ABC News/*Washington Post* poll of Americans found that "64 percent support broader FBI authority to monitor public places such as libraries, places of worship and Internet chat rooms – even though most see this as an intrusion on privacy rights". Obviously Americans were very fearful of another 9/11-type attack.

Meanwhile, as early as 2002, British citizens were concerned about privacy rights. In September of that year a BBC headline appeared: "Terror Laws 'Eat Away at Privacy'". Similar cries have been heard in the United States. How much should the government invade privacy in the name of security?

More taxpayer's money is being spent, more security checks on civilians are carried out, and government officials are asking normal citizens to assist them more to prevent terrorism. The cost of wars fought in far away lands such as Iraq and Afghanistan is very high. Equipping and transporting masses of military personnel and supplies involves huge expense. It is equally expensive to provide homeland security.

Guarding seaport facilities is a major concern. Nations involved in the War on Terror have developed powerful scanning machines. Here, a brown container passes beneath an imaging machine in Baltimore, Maryland, USA. It can take X-ray images through solid steel.

Privacy vs. security

Before 9/11 it was rare for civilians to be searched or otherwise monitored as they are now. People want protection from terrorist attacks, but they also want privacy. There are many questions about how extensively law-abiding citizens should be checked. National identification cards have been proposed in the United States and Britain, and many people have objected to these. They say ID cards are an invasion of privacy, very expensive to organize, and might not even help to prevent terrorist attacks.

Surveillance

An even bigger issue is surveillance. Modern technology makes it possible for government officials to listen to phone conversations and use equipment to listen to people while they are in their own homes. In 2005 President Bush came under harsh criticism when it was revealed that government agents were secretly using such surveillance without warrants or permission from Congress. Bush defended the actions saying they were necessary measures to track terrorists and keep US citizens safe.

Citizens take action

Government leaders have also asked citizens to be active in the search for terrorists. People are to notify authorities if they notice anyone or anything suspicious. Since police and other agents cannot be "everywhere", it is hoped that civilians can assist them in finding terrorists before they take action.

Innocent victims have not only died in huge attacks such as 9/11, but in many other small incidents. Terrorists have sometimes kidnapped holidaymakers, and civilian workers in Iraq have not only been kidnapped, but also executed by terrorists. Changing holiday plans and avoiding places where terrorists operate are other ways people have altered their lifestyles.

Workplaces, schools, government agencies, and the media are all attempting to educate people about the danger of terrorism and to give people suggestions on how to assist in fighting the War on Terror.

EMERGENCY LAW

The Patriot Act went into effect in the United States in October 2001. It gave police and other security officials expanded powers to search, monitor, and investigate suspicious people. The act allows officials to check several types of personal records if there are indications of terrorist behaviour and even allows agents to look at what books a suspect buys. Some people have objected to the Patriot Act on the grounds that it **violates** basic freedoms of speech, press, and privacy rights.

The 2004 Madrid train bombings were some of the worst attacks to ever occur in Spain. They disrupted Spain's national elections, but the terrorists' primary goal was to force Spain to withdraw troops from Iraq.

Bombing Madrid and London

On 11 March 2004 terrorists attacked three of Spain's busiest train stations. Several powerful bombs ripped through carriages of four commuter trains in Madrid during morning rush hour. The bombs killed 190 people and injured over 2,000. The War on Terror had arrived in Spain.

Who and why?

At first, many thought a Spanish group of terrorists had carried out the bombings. Basques, who live in northern Spain, have been pressuring the government for years. Many Basques want their area to become an independent country, and some have resorted to terrorist attacks. However, soon after the bombings, al-Qaeda claimed responsibility. They said they wanted Spanish troops removed from Iraq. Over 70 suspects were arrested and the main bombers were found to be from Morocco.

Spanish Prime Minister José María Aznar, who sent troops to Iraq, was defeated in elections held shortly after the Madrid bombings. The new Prime Minister, Jose Luis Rodriguez Zapatero, who had opposed the war from the beginning, withdrew Spanish forces from Iraq. Many believe that this showed the terrorists had won. However, it may be that the public knew what they were doing in electing a man they knew would withdraw Spanish troops.

London bombed

On 7 July 2005 suicide attackers hit three London Underground trains and one passenger bus. There were 56 people killed and over 700 injured – four of the dead were terrorists. As in Madrid, several of the bombs exploded at almost the same time. Another similarity was that the bombs were set off during a busy time of the morning. Two weeks later, there was a second attempt by terrorists to blow up London trains. In this case, the bombs did not explode and several of the terrorists were captured.

Muslim discontent in Europe

The terrorists in both the London and Madrid bombings appeared to be normal citizens. They were not members of al-Qaeda, but did receive support from the organization. The terrorists were Muslims who apparently became discouraged by several actions of their government leaders.

Years ago, many Muslims moved to European areas for job opportunities, but in recent years the economies have changed. There is higher unemployment and this has hit Muslims living in Europe very hard. Combined with opposition to the war in Iraq, some frustrated European Muslims have been encouraged by al-Qaeda to carry out terrorist attacks.

MUSLIM DISCONTENT IN EUROPE

In October 2005, two teenage Muslims living in France were accidentally killed. Reports were that the two youths ran away from police and tragically died when they touched live electrical connections. Many Muslims believed the two were unfairly targeted and this sparked huge riots in France. Many wonder if the large population of discontented, poor Muslims who live in European nations such as France will cause more terrorist attacks like those in London and Madrid.

Britain has installed many surveillance cameras. One took this photo in a London underground station. It shows four terrorists responsible for the London bombings on 7 July 2005. Unfortunately, they were not identified as terrorists until after the attacks.

Can terrorism be stopped?

Some people say that terrorism cannot be stopped. Despite the United States being the most powerful nation in the world, it has struggled to win the War on Terror. Large armies are of little use against individuals and small groups that carry out terrorist acts. It is also extremely expensive to guard and inspect potential terrorist targets: crowded areas, and land, air, and sea vehicles are all good targets for terrorism.

Threats?

The mission in Iraq may take years, but other areas may also be targeted by the United States. Bush included North Korea in his "**axis of evil**" because it has nuclear weapons and has made threats to take over South Korea – a nation under US protection. North Korea is not specifically a target of the War on Terror. The United States believes Iran is responsible for organizing and supporting terrorist attacks, and there is substantial evidence to support this. Iran now has nuclear technology and many of the world's nations are concerned that it will produce nuclear weapons.

Congressional opposition

Opposition to President Bush strengthened in the United States during 2005. Members of the US Congress began to express concerns that the United States will be unable to exit from Iraq without continued high casualties. They have also doubted that US assistance will result in a stable, united Iraqi government. The costs of the mission in Iraq and the reasons for going to war in the first place have also been questioned.

On the Canadian–US border, a security officer checks a traveller's passport. New US laws have been passed to help prevent terrorists from entering the country. Non-US citizens now have to give fingerprints and be photographed when they arrive.

Special forces units were used to track down the terrorists involved in the London bombings on 7 and 21 July 2005.

A long war

It appears that the War on Terror will be a long one. Special-forces units play important roles in finding and capturing suspected terrorists. Several countries are asking their citizens to help prevent terrorist acts by staying vigilant and reporting any suspicious-looking people.

Just as police constantly study the methods of criminals and find new techniques to deal with them, nations must better understand and properly deal with terrorists. It is possible that several new measures will be taken, such as more metal detectors in public buildings, more limitations on personal privacy to track terrorists. Those who become experts on terrorism need to share their knowledge to prevent problems such as wars and the negative effects on the economies of nations that are victims of terrorism.

WAR WITH IRAN NEXT?

There is a great amount of evidence that Iran has provided funds and support for terrorist groups. The country is led by strict Shi'ite Muslims and they have been strongly opposed to US policies and lifestyles for several years. Now that they admit possessing nuclear technology, President Bush has issued several warnings and asked that international inspectors examine nuclear sites. Many countries fear Iran could be the next location for war.

Experts speak about terrorism

Nations all over the world are working hard to stop terrorism. World leaders include the problem of terrorism in virtually every conversation they have with each other. Experts from around the world are being asked how best to deal with terrorists.

Fighting terrorist wars

Fighting terrorists is very different from fighting a conventional war. Large armies and powerful weapons have limited success when their opponents fight in small scattered bands that can easily hide. In fact, large military forces make easy targets for terrorists, who look like friendly civilians right up to the time they attack.

US Congressman Jim Turner identified three main tasks to win the War on Terror: 1. Identify and locate terrorist enemies through global collection and sharing of intelligence; 2. Take the battle to the terrorists, wherever they may be, by cutting off their sources of financing; 3. improve relations with the people who live in the same nations where terrorists hide. He concluded: "If countries understand and help each other progress, they will help each other fight the War on Terror too."

Loren Thompson, a military operations expert in Arlington, Virginia, USA, says that technology has limitations. He points out that all technology, such as sensors, spy aircraft, and satellite communications, does "is move information around, but the information itself is the key to victory". He says that "old-fashioned tips from humans" are more important in finding and defeating the enemy.

Perhaps the best peacemakers are individuals from different countries who simply help others. Here, a British medic treats a young Iraqi child in March 2003.

Secret missions

Paul Wilkinson, a Scottish expert on terrorism, says that using the phrase "war on terrorism" is understandable after 9/11, "but if you use a phrase like that, it does create an expectation among some people that there is a solution to terrorism that is entirely military". He says the best way to stop terrorism is "by the less glamorous, less dramatic form of counter-terrorism – through intelligence, good intelligence-sharing, getting such good information on the intentions and plans of the group that you can intervene before they carry out their attacks".

Henry Kissinger is a former US secretary of state and winner of a Nobel Peace Prize. Many recent presidents have sought his opinions. The world's governments now look to such experts for advice in handling the problem of terrorism.

ARABS OPPOSING TERRORISM

Leaders throughout the world know there is much to learn in order to effectively deal with terrorists. In February 2005 Crown Prince Abdullah, an important national leader in Saudi Arabia, organized an anti-terrorism conference in his nation. Representatives of 50 countries attended and shared ideas. In his speech, Amr Moussa, Secretary-General of the **Arab League**, said that "confronting terror cannot be done individually". He asserted that the international community needs to work together to win the War on Terror.

What do you think?

Some people say the media should tell more about the progress being made in the War on Terror. Others say the media should be doing more to help stop the violence associated with the war. What do you think?

- Is the media of your country accurately and fairly reporting the War on Terror?

The 9/11 attacks were the main reason that the United States declared the War on Terror. Many terrorist suspects were captured and put in prisons. The United States has attempted to find out where other terrorists are by using various methods. Some people say they tortured prisoners of war.

- Should other methods like secret missions to find terrorists have been used rather than going to war?

- Should mild forms of torture be used on prisoners if they tell questioners important anti-terrorist information, and therefore save innocent lives?

Many measures have been taken to protect civilians from terrorist attacks. No terrorist attacks have occurred in the United States since 9/11, but major attacks have affected Britain, Indonesia, Australia, and Spain.

- Will terrorist attacks increase or decrease in these nations in the next five years? In the next 20 years?

- Do you agree with the security measures being taken in your country? What more could be done?

Years after the wars in Afghanistan and Iraq started, the United States, Britain, and Australia still had troops stationed in those nations. The wars were costly to all nations involved.

- Was the US-led Coalition correct in going to war with Afghanistan and Iraq when it did?

- Is the world safer today than it was at the time of 9/11?

Everyone needs to work together to prevent terrorism. As terrorism is dealt with, an even bigger issue looms – understanding each other so we can live in peace. Meanwhile, the media has responsibility for providing news that is accurate and free of one-sided opinions.

TERRORISM VS. CONVENTIONAL WAR

Scottish expert Paul Wilkinson says: "I always point out that although terrorism is an evil and lots of people unfortunately lose their lives – including many civilians – through terrorism, it is not as terrible an evil as major wars in which hundreds of thousands and possibly millions can be killed. We have to be very careful that we do not bring about those wider and more terrible conflicts of potential mass annihilation in the process of trying to suppress terrorism. That would be a tragic folly."

The War on Terror is the subject of much debate. Will you be able to judge whether the media is telling the truth?

TIMELINE

February 1993

Al-Qaeda terrorists detonate a bomb in the United States under New York City's World Trade Center. Despite damage, the skyscraper's basic structure is not compromised.

October 1993

Two US helicopters shot down in Somalia, killing 18 soldiers. US officials believe that al-Qaeda helped to train those responsible.

June 1996

A bomb explodes in a US military housing complex in Saudi Arabia, killing 19 Americans.

October 1997

UN Disarmament Commission says Iraq is concealing information on chemical weapons and missiles.

January 1998

Iraq ends all cooperation with UN weapons inspectors.

February 1998

Osama Bin Laden issues a statement calling for more attacks on American targets around the world.

August 1998

More than 220 people are killed when bombs explode in the US embassies in Kenya and Tanzania. The United States retaliate with airstrikes against alleged al-Qaeda training camps in Sudan and Afghanistan.

October 2000

Two suicide bombers attack the USS *Cole* in Yemen, killing 17 sailors.

September 2001

Al-Qaeda terrorists destroy the World Trade Center and damage the Pentagon in Washington, D.C. Around 3,000 people are killed.

September 2001

US President George W. Bush declares War on Terror.

October 2001

War with Afghanistan begins.

October 2002
Two explosions kill 202 people in nightclubs in Bali, Indonesia.

November 2002
UN weapons inspectors return to Iraq, but are hindered by Iraqi officials and cannot make proper inspections.

March 2003
War in Iraq begins.

April 2003
War in Iraq is declared a victory for Coalition forces, but violence continues.

August 2003
Explosion destroys UN headquarters in Iraq – 24 people are killed.

March 2004
Trains in Madrid, Spain, are bombed by terrorists – 191 people are killed, and 1,400 are injured.

April 2004
Abuse of prisoners at Abu Ghraib prison in Iraq is revealed.

September 2004
Over 300 civilians, including 186 children, are killed when a hostage situation ends in a violent shoot-out in Russia.

January 2005
Iraqi elections are held and a huge number of voters participate despite attacks on election day meant to discourage voters.

March 2005
Italian journalist Giuliana Sgrena is accidentally wounded by US soldiers as she rides to freedom. She had been held hostage since February.

July 2005
Three London Underground trains and one passenger bus are bombed by terrorists – 56 people are killed, and over 700 are injured. Two weeks later, bombs fail to detonate in a second attack.

2006
Polls show public confidence in President Bush is decreasing due to continued deaths of US personnel in Iraq.

GLOSSARY

administration the management of a government

allies countries that help another country for a military or other purpose

al-Qaeda terrorist organization that has made several attacks on the United States and European nations. Responsible for the 9/11 attacks.

Arab League group of Arab nations who work together politically and economically

axis of evil term used to describe governments that sponsor terrorism

bias for or against a particular viewpoint. For example, an article can be biased towards a particular political party.

Coalition name for the group of nations united to defeat Saddam Hussein's forces

Congress the US Congress is composed of the Senate and the House of Representatives

conventional war conflict fought by normal methods of warfare

culture attitudes and behaviour of a particular social group

democratic government organized system of laws where citizens can vote for their leaders

disunity disagreement and conflict within a group

embedded reporter person researching a story by accompanying an active military unit

exiled forced to leave one's homeland because of a serious crime or offence

extremist person who holds extreme views, particularly one who uses violence to advocate the views

free election election where people are free to vote without fear of intimidation or corruption

guerilla soldier who fights using secret attacks, usually part of a small unit

hijack illegally take control of a vehicle

hostage person being held against his or her will

insurgency uprising against a source of authority

Islam religion based on the teachings of Muhammad

jihad holy war fought in the name of Islam

Kurds group of people living in northern Iraq and southern Turkey that have a common culture

legislation laws of a state or country

media sources that report news including TV, radio, newspapers, and magazines

mobilize prepare and organize troops for a war

Muslims followers of Islam

nationalism intense belief that one's native country is best

objective representing facts without personal opinions or bias

Persian Gulf War 1991 war led by the United States and various European and Middle Eastern allies, against Iraqi occupation of Kuwait

retraction official correction made in newspaper or other publication

sceptical not easily convinced

Shi'ite Muslims followers of Islam who base their beliefs on the teachings of Muhammad and his relative, Ali

special forces military units with particular skills and training so they can be used for specific missions

suicide car bombs vehicles filled with explosives that are crashed into a target, causing damage and killing the driver

suicide mission terrorist act where the detonation of explosives will result in the death of the bomber

Sunni Muslims followers of Islam who base their beliefs primarily on teachings of Muhammad and Islamic leaders who gained control after his death

surveillance secretly observing others to gain information

Taliban extremist Muslim group that seized control of Afghanistan's government in 1996 and ruled until 2001

violate break or fail to comply with a rule or agreement

Western culture the modern culture of western Europe and North America

FIND OUT MORE

Further reading

Inside the World's Most Infamous Terrorist Organizations: Egyptian Islamic Jihad, Phillip Marguiles
(Rosen, 2004)

September 11, 2001, Brendan January
(Heinemann Library, 2003)

The Bombing of London 2005, Andrew Langley
(Raintree, 2006)

The Crisis of Islam: Holy War and Unholy Terror, Bernard Lewis
(Phoenix Press, 2004)

Troubled World: Arab-Israeli Conflict, Ivan Minnis
(Heinemann Library, 2001)

Troubled World: Saddam Hussein and Iraq, David Downing
(Heinemann Library, 2004)

Understanding September 11th: Answering Questions about the Attacks on America, Mitch Frank
(Viking, 2002)

Witness to History: Afghanistan, David Downing
(Heinemann Library, 2004)

Witness to History: The War in Iraq, David Downing
(Heinemann Library, 2004)

Websites

news.bbc.co.uk
Keep up with the latest developments with a news website such as this one.

www.whitehouse.gov/infocus/nationalsecurity/index.html
The US Government's opinion on any developments in the War on Terror can be found on this website. You can also watch videos of important speeches.

www.defendamerica.mil
News from the US Department of Defense can be read here.

www.army.mil/terrorism
This timeline, showing the history of terrorist attacks around the world, has been produced by the US Army.

www.amnestyusa.org/waronterror/index.do
The Amnesty International USA website contains fascinating articles about how the War on Terror has affected human rights.

www.cfr.org/issue/135
The Council on Foreign Relations is an independent organization dedicated to producing and disseminating ideas and information dregarding US foreign policy.

Activities

Here are some topics to research if you want to find out more about the War on Terror:

- counterterrorism strategies

- freedom of speech

- the First Amendment of the US Constitution

- the World Trade Center bombing of 1993

- Adam Curtis' documentary, *The Power of Nightmares*.

INDEX

Titles in the *Behind the News* series include:

Hardback   0-431-11471-4

Hardback   0-431-11472-2

Hardback   0-431-11473-0

Hardback   0-431-11474-9

Hardback   0-431-11475-7

Find out about other titles from Heinemann Library on our website www.heinemann.co.uk/library